Identity

Identity

WHO DO YOU THINK YOU ARE?

As A Man Thinketh So Is He

ROBERT JOHNSON & ANGELA KINNEL

Robert L. Johnson

Religion

Book Cover Design Robert Johnson & Jcovers
Special thanks to editors Robyn Norwood and Debra Johnson
Contact:www.bloodboughtpromises.com
For worldwide distribution, Printed in the USA

ISBN 978-0-9860180-1-5
0-9860180-1-5

DEDICATION

This book is dedicated to my family for their consistent support and encouragement. Ever since the day I revealed the call on my life to you, you've had my back with no hesitation. I thank God for you…Stella Kinnel, Edward Kinnel Sr. and Edward Kinnel Jr. To my oldest brother, the late LaNoris W. Kinnel, I hope that you're proud of me!

Angela Kinnel

This book is dedicated to my wife, family, friends, and everyone that listened. Thank you for your continued encouragement and support. Thank you also to Achieving Excellence Toastmasters Club at WCCI for helping me to find my voice. I love you all, be blessed!

Robert Johnson

Table of Contents

PREFACE

This book is for anyone who has suffered with feelings of guilt or shame because they missed the mark. If you've ever felt as though you're not good enough or you don't measure up or that your righteousness lies within your works, then hold on. This book is for you! We know the difference God's perspective has on how we view ourselves and what we ultimately accomplish while on the earth.

Your true identity will set you free from the deception that has kept you from receiving Gods best. Don't deny yourself the opportunity to see what God has in store for you. Grab on to your identity and be who you were called to be in Christ. For God so loved the world He gave His only begotten Son that you may be free, and in Christ we are free indeed.

> ² *Don't copy the behavior and customs of this world, but let God transform you into a new person by changing the way you think. Then you will learn to know God's will for you, which is good and pleasing and perfect. Romans 12:2 (NLT)*

INTRODUCTION

We count ourselves blessed because you have chosen to read *Identity (Who do you think you are?)*. We pray your soul be edified as you take this journey into true self-discovery. Our deepest desire as we walk through the Word of God is that your self-perception will conform to the image of Christ, and that you will be encouraged to see yourself as God sees you.

> *In all things we are more than conquerors through Him that loved us. Romans 8:37*

At various times in life we have both been faced with identity crisis. We have both suffered scrutiny. We have endured negative opinions, and verbal curses others have taken liberty to spew at us. Many of the things said and lessons learned contributed to how we viewed ourselves; unfortunately the impact of this was negative and designed by Satan to prevent us from grasping the truth of our identity in Christ.

Identity

In past times if someone addressed me as a "man of God" it actually made me quite uncomfortable which seems strange to me now. Back then, because of religious teaching my idea of a "man of God" was based in works. My identity complex wouldn't allow me to see beyond my personal failures and short comings, so there was no way I could wear that title "man of God" without shame; I knew who I was primarily because everyone had told me.

I just couldn't see myself as a man of God. Allow me to give clarity, I accepted Christ as my personal Lord and Savior, I was baptized, attended church regularly and even worked in a Christian bookstore. However, in spite of the religious teaching I heard; the criticisms, negative observations and guilt, prevented me from seeing myself accurately. I viewed myself from the vantage point of my failures. I viewed myself through the eyes of others . . . a dangerous posture to assume.

I needed a change of perspective and I had no way of achieving that without looking outside of my immediate environment. If something hadn't changed I would have been stuck with a self-image destined to bring a life of frustration and failure. As I began to pray and seek God, the message of Grace was presented to me. It was as though a light came on in my spirit and mind. That's who I really am. I'm in Christ and He's in me, we are now one.

> *I and the Father are one John 10:30*

My life changed forever. No longer did I view myself through the perceptions of others, or according to my works. I learned that my Identity was that of Jesus Christ and that everything He is, I am before God.

> *But the person who is joined to the Lord is one spirit with Him. 1*

Wow! That was so liberating I can't put it into words. We took a spiritual journey through the Gospel of Grace and our lives were forever changed. Through the pages of this book we invite you to take the same journey of self-discovery in Christ.

Chapter 1

WHO ARE YOU?

Many of us battle with this question because deep down we know we are many people and perhaps even many things depending on who is asked. Most of us have worn so many different labels that our true identity may have gotten lost in the definitions, opinions and perspectives of others. Believe it or not there is no shortage of people willing to shape and mold our self-perception and identity.

They are more than happy to project various limitations into our hearts and minds regarding our identity, people often attempt to direct how we see ourselves with their words and actions. It's not at all unusual that we tend to see ourselves as others see us. Many Sociologists agree that an individual's identity is formed primarily by initial contacts, usually our parents and those we interact with most.

Some say our identities are most influenced by our environment, our neighborhoods and communities. Others say it is our experiences that will most impact our identity and how we view ourselves. No doubt all of the things are important parts of how our identity is formed. However, we believe you can purposefully choose to believe and identify with the Creator's view of your identity in Christ. We believe that as we began to better understand the word of God regarding who we are and what we can do, then we will do all things. It is Jesus the Christ who provides this new and true identity.

> In this [union and fellowship with Him], love is completed and perfected with us, so that we may have confidence in the day of judgment [with assurance and boldness to face Him]; because as He is, so are we in this world . 1 John 4:17 (AMP)

What is identity?

To understand how identity is formed (*in the natural*); we must first grasp what identity really is. Simply put, identity defines who an individual is. It is forged through a process of development of uniqueness. However, "Identity is a multifaceted concept – it relates to the understandings and ideas people hold about who they are and what is meaningful to them" (Giddens 76). According to Giddens, the concept of identity consists of two major components. This is why sociologists classify the term (*identity*) into social identity and self-identity. "Social identity" compiles the characteristics other people attribute to an individual. Conversely, self-identity refers to the process of self-development; states Marvin Lee in his 2012 Article (*How Identity is formed*).

Erik Erikson (Theories of Identity) states, "Identity provides one with a sense of wellbeing, a sense of being at home in one's body, a sense of direction in one's life, and a sense of mattering to those who count." (Erikson, 1968). That's a lot of info and it appears to be correct for the most part. Everyone wants a feeling of wellbeing and everyone wants to be comfortable in their own skin. However, what stood out most to us was the last part of Erikson's statement, "Identity provided a sense of direction in life and a sense of mattering to those who count." It's pretty important to note that in essence, an inaccurate view of our identity can mislead our direction in life. Where we look for our identity becomes a matter of good life or death. So what's the source of your identity?

Family and Friends

As we began to think about writing our experiences, observations, and lessons we thought it best to begin with family and friends, for they are very influential in how we began to form our natural identity. Most of us grew up taking cues from those around us. For good or bad they began the process of how we would view ourselves and how we would identify ourselves. As it regards family it is probably the most influential group where early identity formation is concerned. Most of us have relatives that were role models and authority figures and when they spoke it meant something. For whatever reason we believed what they told us, perhaps it was the fact that we had no other sources of information or maybe it was just conditioning. But whatever it was had impact and what they said became the foundation of our beliefs. I don't believe that relatives set out to miseducate and limit us. I think in most cases they just didn't know themselves, they didn't have clear revelation on the word of God, so they taught what they knew.

They didn't know how important it was to watch what they said to and about us, they didn't understand the power of words. They had no idea that in some cases they were pronouncing curses over our lives on a daily basis. They thought reminding you of your family's failures was just a cautionary tale, something that would help you to avoid the pitfalls, but instead in most cases it just made you self-conscience. It didn't seem to matter what the issue was, whether a sickness that seems to be hereditary or some bad habit that has plagued the family, you were going to get it. People were quick to tell you that high blood pressure just runs in our family or that poverty is our destiny because God wants you to be happy later, when you get to heaven. The expectations that we had for life were often framed by these limiting beliefs. But the bible teaches that we can do all things through Christ that strengthens us, we are free from the curse of limitations.

Friends are also influential, but as you can see, one group we inherit and the other we get to choose. Oddly enough we often select friends based on who we believe ourselves to be, even if who we believe ourselves to be has been determined by someone else. If everyone tells you "you are dumb" then you will most likely select friends you have something in common with. It is an unfortunate fact and this is why knowledge of your identity is so important. Developing the proper identity and attitude is contingent upon what we hear, what we say and what we focus on.

> *My dear friends, don't believe everything you hear. Carefully weigh and examine what people tell you. 1 John 4:1 (Msg)*

Through experience we have learned there is often conflict between who we believe we are and who others perceive us to be. What we choose to believe will either cause failure or success in reaching our potential.

> *"There is a way which seems right to a man, but its end is the way of death." Proverbs 16:25*

It is a sad fact that most of us don't give much thought to how we've become who we've become. We have not considered the multitude of people and ideas that have influenced our attitudes, tolerances, philosophies, values and habits. Most of us wander through life reacting and responding to the events of life as if we're on auto-pilot. We rarely seem to think about exactly what we are thinking about, against the back drop of truth according to The Word of God.

> *We are destroying sophisticated arguments and every exalted and proud thing that sets itself up against the [true] knowledge of God, and we are taking every thought and purpose captive to the obedience of Christ. 2 Corinthians 10:5 (AMP)*

Until we developed identity issues of our own, we never gave much thought to the positive and negative influence our family and friends had on our self-perception!   It's difficult to

5

determine whether a mean or malicious statement toward a child is any worse than not being present to say anything at all. These are often the experiences that shape our concepts of value and identity. We know that one of the most precious gifts we were given is free will; the power to choose. We get to choose how we define ourselves and where to draw our identity from.

> *"Today I have given you the choice between life and death, between blessings and curses. Now I call on heaven and earth to witness the choice you make. Oh, that you would choose life, so that you and your descendants might live!" Deuteronomy 30:19*

Many of us need a good godly brain washing because our memories are filthy with the residue of failure and the shame of wrong choices and missed opportunities. Too often we view ourselves as the sum total of our results. Many of us believe that if we tried and failed we are a failure. That if someone ceased to love us, we believe we are unlovable. The world philosophy believes we are what we do; no more, and no less however, that is not Gods perspective.

> *Therefore being justified by faith, we have peace with God through our Lord Jesus Christ: Romans 5:1*

Environment

It would be extremely difficult to discuss identity without consideration for the environment whereby our sense of identity is developed. Many of us did not have the luxury of a two-parent or a two-income household. Many of us weren't an extension of a community we could be proud of nor did we have a zip code that demanded respect. Many of us saw our environment as something to be ashamed of as well. I grew up on the south side of Chicago and remained there a total of thirty years. Along with that geographical location came several forgone conclusions. A few of those conclusions determined I would be dead or in prison by age thirty, I would likely have a group of children I wouldn't care for, and would end up a loser. (Those were not my thoughts.)

Though my father was absent I knew that if I ever had children I would be to them a father that was everything that mine wasn't. I refused to shape my identity by my environment or what people believed to be my most likely outcome. Although Angela and I were both raised in church there was no talk of identity other than we were labeled sinners saved by grace. I was convinced that at any moment Jesus might take my salvation back if I sinned just one more time. It was petrifying. No one told us to take our focus off of our attempts to keep the Law. Much of the time our worst view of self came from the area of misconstrued beliefs about God, and church, because we knew we were coming up short most of the time.

That kind of legalistic environment will cause anyone to view themselves in the worst way possible; condemned, unworthy and unrighteous. With that as our identity we were powerless to view ourselves accurately. Remember, we get to decide what type of environment we remain in, yet without Christ we have no point of reference to determine where we should be. In Christ your spirit will become more sensitive to the truth of

God and your faith will soar. It's in Christ only that the proper environment exists to reach our God given potential. It is Jesus Christ in us who brings the power and gives us our identity. The power in you in Christ and Christ is the hope of glory.

> "Christ in you, the hope of glory" *Colossians 1:27*

Experiences

We have all had experiences that have propelled us to a place of faith, hope and possibility. Likewise, we have felt the sting of a dream destroyed by words of defeat and failure. In both instances, someone was involved in shaping that experience, and in either instance there is a proper response as it regards our identity. Issues, failures and problem situations often have a great impact on who we believe we are.

> *For as a man thinketh in his heart so is he. Proverbs 23:7*

If we have experienced loss or failed to experience a desired effect through our efforts we have a tendency to view ourselves in the context of our shortcomings. Society reinforces the mindset that having failed in a particular area makes one a failure and if we don't resist that concept we will see ourselves through the eyes of the world.

> *No, dear brothers and sisters, I have not achieved it, but I focus on this one thing: <u>Forgetting the past and looking forward to what lies ahead,</u> Philippians 3:13 (NLT)*

The problem here is that once we've adopted that philosophy we become the picture we see and it takes refocusing to place our identity in its proper perspective. We must see ourselves as God sees us in order to have a mindset that frees us from the shame and despair associated with failure. How then does a person essentially change who they are in their mind? Well, the word of God tells us that it is not only possible to do this, but it instructs us on how to do it.

> *Don't copy the behavior and customs of this world, but <u>let God transform you into a new person by changing the way you think</u>. Then you will learn to know God's will for you, which is good and pleasing and perfect. Romans 12:2 (NLT)*

Renewing the mind is the process of exchanging what you currently believe with the truth of God's Word. Let's be honest. Although many of us have no idea how we came to think as we do, the Bible definitely does.

> *So then faith cometh by hearing, and hearing by the word of God.*
> *Romans 10:17*

In effect what we are hearing is shaping our ideas, philosophies and ultimately our identity itself. The process begins with the hearing. If the environment we dwell in most is speaking contrary to the Word of God, we will develop ideas and perspectives that are in opposition to God's view of our identity. God, the creator of all, has instructed us to not be influenced by what we see. This includes our shortcomings and faults. We are to walk in such faith that we can operate as God has described in His word.

> *For we walk by faith, not by sight: 2 Corinthians 5:7*

I know many of us look at our experiences, actions and results and think "it is what it is". We feel powerless to see ourselves as successful, delivered, righteous, and justified. However, in Christ that is how God sees us; faultless. As we continue to show sensitivity in how we view our experiences we will began to see that it's not our experiences that determine the outcome; but the experiences of Jesus that determine our outcome. We must take every negative thought and replace it with The Word. God truly loves us. He desires that we renew our mind in The Word and begin to allow the word to show us a picture of ourselves and the faith and confidence necessary to manifest our identity. As we look to the word to define us it will develop and reshape our thinking, our direction and our destiny.

> *In all thy ways acknowledge him, and he shall direct thy paths. Proverbs 3:6*

Chapter 2

HOW DO YOU KNOW?

Based on the insight we've taken from science and The Word of God regarding how identity is formed, we are compelled to question how much of this information came from God, and how much has come from society. It is imperative we have a good understanding of what is at stake here. There is a battle taking place over your mind. Make no mistake. Someone or something is always attempting to influence your identity and destiny.

The world's message of value and worth is rooted in misleading philosophies that ultimately lead us into a world of self-deception; believing who we are now is who we will always be. Sayings such as" a leopard can't change its spots" are mainstream. Considering this saying, what if you were never a leopard. What if someone had only convinced you that you were a leopard and now they were trying to convince you that because you're a leopard; you can't identify with change because leopards don't change. In spite of this tactic you realize you were never a leopard, you can shake off the limitations that bind leopards. So how do you know you're not that leopard or weak powerless person? How do you overcome the stigma associated with that idea of yourself? How do we get beyond what the world has drilled in our heads for thousands of years? How will we know the truth about our identity?

Well first and foremost we must have the truth of God in order to detect a lie of the world. As mentioned the world's message of value and worth is rooted in misleading philosophies that ultimately lead us into self-deception. This is God's message to believers (*I see you as I see Jesus*), Fear not. All is well.

> *22 throw off your old sinful nature and your former way of life, which is corrupted by lust and deception. 23 Instead, let the Spirit renew your thoughts and attitudes. 24 Put on your new nature, created to be like God—truly righteous and holy.*
> Ephesians 4:22-24 (NLT)

The world's message

The world as we know it can be a most deceptive place. Nearly every waking moment is filled with constant assaults on our thought lives, our decisions and our identity itself. According to Joe Flint of the Los Angeles Times, we see an average 15 minutes of commercial advertising during every one hour program we watch. Can you guess why? Because each ad is there to shape and form our thought process, decisions and identity. What's worse is the fact that the new trend is to jam even more messages into that one hour program, placing more commercials in the same 15 minutes? Advertisers have come to understand that one of the most effective ways to manipulate the public is to send shorter more directed messages. They understand that all that is necessary to prompt acceptance of a product, idea or service is a strong 15 second seed and a receptive viewer.

However, everything that is jockeying for dominance over our thought lives is not on television. What we hear repeatedly, what we read and even pictures in books, magazines and the internet have an incredible impact on our values, view points and self-perception. It is true we are bombarded on all sides by information designed to create appetites and philosophies counter-productive to discovering our identity in Christ.

Might I add that our most common source of misleading and misidentification are those closest to us; those we know and in some cases love, but we'll get to that in a moment. For now, our focus is the messages the world so desperately wants all of us to accept. I do think it's worth noting that our point of reference is crucial to distinguishing between the messages that help us to see things properly and the messages that don't. For instance, we have witnessed firsthand the message of marriage being distorted. We have witnessed a redefining of marriage by those who wish to direct our thinking to align with theirs. If an individual has no biblical point of reference all they're left with to determine a good or bad message is how you feel about the matter. We should all acknowledge that how we feel about a matter is a terrible foundation upon which to make a decision, adopt a philosophy or determine our identity. Why not you say? Well, the answer is feelings are subject to change. As a matter of fact by the time you're done reading this book we pray you feel differently and moreover we pray you believe differently.

> *Then we will no longer be immature like children. We won't be tossed and blown about by every wind of new teaching.* <u>*We will not be influenced when people try to trick us with lies so clever they sound like the truth.*</u> *Ephesians 4:14 (NLT)*

The world has devised many tools to tell us if we're winners or losers, smart or dumb, attractive or ugly, educated or illiterate. The world will even determine your chances of success or failure based on pedigree, race, and economic situations. Society will analyze where you're from and even how many parents were in your household, to predict your value, worth and likelihood of success. This is all based on worldly standards.

You see, the message of the world always aims to define us and redesign our thinking to fit their plans and purposes. We've all fallen prey to the spin doctors from time to time. I can recall ads that flat out told me if I didn't drive a particular car then people would view me (negatively).

However if I drove their car I would be popular, sexy and every woman would want me, and desire to ride with such an accomplished man. We've also heard that if we wear designer clothes and lived in a certain place we are a success. On the contrary if we didn't have designer wear and didn't live in a certain place we weren't a success.

Please don't misunderstand. There's nothing wrong with having nice things, driving nice cars and wearing nice clothes (we should). But, this should have no bearing on your self-perception or your identity. This idea that I am as people perceive me is a dangerous idea. Of course it feels good as long as their view of you is positive, but not so much when they view you differently, which by the way is a by-product of how they feel about you. As we stated previously, feelings are fragile and subject to change. We as believers can't depend on limited view-points or material things to empower our identity.

God is the source of our identity and it is our responsibility to discover our identity in Christ through the Word of God, not through the eyes of others or the world's message. If you think about it the identity of any creation is determined by its creator. If you want to know the truth about any product, idea, service or philosophy, what better source to consult than the creator? Likewise, God is our creator and He is completely aware of who we are, what we can do and how we should identify ourselves.

> So *God created man in his own image*, in the image of God created he him; male and female created he them.
> *Genesis 1:27*

It's up to us to read the manual; the Word of God and apply His principles to get His results. You must believe in something; either the message of the world or what God says about you. Many of us have not given much thought to why we believe what we believe but as we begin to think about what we're thinking about it is important we get to the origin of our thoughts. We get to choose what we believe. We've all heard things we have chosen not to believe based on the information itself or the credibility of the messenger, but for whatever reason we chose not to believe. Identity is no different. The information in the Word of God is both good and credible and it's a picture of who we are in Christ.

> *And if it seem evil unto you to serve the LORD, <u>choose you this day whom ye will serve</u>; Joshua 24:15*

Our prayer is that we will all choose Christ as the source of our identity and in our discovery, we will be who He says we are; more than a conquerors.

> *What, then, shall we say in response to these things? If God is for us, who can be against us? 32 He who did not spare his own Son, but gave him up for us all—how will he not also, along with him, graciously give us all things? 33 Who will bring any charge against those whom God has chosen? <u>It is God who justifies.</u> 34 Who then is the one who condemns? No one. Christ Jesus who died—more than that, who was raised to life—is at the right hand of God and is also interceding for us. 35 Who shall separate us from the love of Christ? Shall trouble or hardship or persecution or famine or nakedness or danger or sword? Romans 8:31-35 NIV No, <u>in all these things we are more than conquerors through him who loved us.</u> 38 For I am convinced that neither death nor life, neither angels nor demons, neither the present nor the future, nor any powers, 39 neither height nor depth, <u>nor anything else in all creation, will be able to separate us from the love of God that is in Christ Jesus our Lord.</u> 8:37-39 (NIV)*

Deception

> *And Jesus answered and said to them, "See to it that no one misleads you." Matthew 24:4*

Merriam-Webster defines deception as the act of *making someone believe something that is not true;* that act of deceiving someone. Also, it's a statement intended to *make people believe something that is not true.* Wow! Based on this definition, it is clear that deception can be a dangerous and in some cases a life altering thing. Clearly deception can come in many forms. Sometimes deception is in what's said. At other times it can be displayed in what is omitted. Some deception is rather harmless and in some cases serves a logical purpose. For instance, when you want to surprise someone with a birthday party a little deception and omission is necessary to keep the birthday secret, however aside from that deception rarely brings joy.

It appears that some form of deception is always lurking in plain sight, to mislead and misdirect. Why is deception used so much and why are so many people deceived? Why would anyone work night and day thinking of ways to deceive us. Why is that so important? Well, in most cases if a person deceives you it is normally toward some end that benefits them versus you. The entire point of deception is to gain some upper hand over those being deceived and then to use that advantage to extract whatever ransom they desire.

Some deception is designed to convince us that what we know to be true is not true (as with Eve in the garden of Eden) Some deception is vice versa, and an attempt to convince you to believe lies as with Job (he was convinced that God had behaved unfairly). Either way, the endgame is the same. To hide or manipulate the truth. Most deception is substitutionary, that is to say it seeks not only to say something is not true, but also seeks to replace the truth with a lie as in for example, (God did not create the world and mankind); it was the (Big Bang and evolution). Why would it benefit men to perpetuate the lie of Big Bang and evolution as the origin of this earth and mankind. Why would anyone pursue that as a lifelong quest? I can see but one purpose for such deception and that would be to discredit Jehovah God the Creator of all.

Now, in keeping with deception being designed to give an undue advantage what is the advantage being pursued by discrediting God? Well, if Satan can use people to discredit the Word of God which clearly states that *In the beginning God created the Heavens and the Earth Genesis 1:1*

Then in effect Satan is using men to call God a liar. God is not a man and cannot lie.

> *God is not a man that He should lie; Numbers 23:19*

It's really interesting that when science speaks of evolution the only people who get angry are people who believe in God. In truth I would think that the Satanist should be angry as well, because Satan was first introduced to mankind in the Word of God. If the Bible is untrue then the attack is not only against God but Satan as well. This appears as a paradox but it is not, because Satan is fine with us believing he doesn't exist. Believing that he does not exist has no impact on his plans to destroy us; as a matter of fact it enhances his opportunities. However, on the other hand the absence of God will have an enormous impact on mankind in general and on all people of God in particular.

All deception is bad but this level of deception has tremendous consequences because Satan seeks to discredit God through the use of humanism as a substitute. If he is successful mankind will constantly look at themselves to define what's right and wrong, what's fair or unfair, what's good or bad and most importantly what's true or untrue. If Satan can convince us that it's all made up then we won't attempt to pursue God for knowledge and wisdom, or an accurate picture of our identity according to the Word of God. Just think about it. No one is looking for unicorns because we've all conceded that they don't exist. When man buys into the concept that he defines himself apart from God then Satan has him right where he wants him. He can then begin the slow and meticulous process of shaping and forming our beliefs, our convictions, and ultimately our identities.

I've often told my children I refuse to send them into the world with an empty cup, meaning there are values and principles that I must instill into them before they leave my house and go out into a world full of deception. They needed to know who they were in Christ, what they could expect in Christ and why they believe in Christ before they left my house. I knew that if they were firm in who they really are in Christ they would reach the heights God called them to. If they were not certain of who they were, (what they could do, and who had their back) then people would try to fill the cup with whatever most served their agenda.

For those of us who believe in Jesus, rightly dividing the word of truth is the key to decoding our identity. Failure to do so has consequences that will lead to frustration and unbelief.

> *But when He, the Spirit of truth, comes, He will guide you into all the truth; for He will not speak on His own initiative, but whatever He hears, He will speak; and He will disclose to you what is to come. John 16:13*

If we miss it we will wander through life adopting deception as identity never reaching our appointed destination. I used to have a poster on the wall at my office and it read "if you have no destination in mind it matters not what road you take". A purposeful trip begins with a destination in mind. We don't want to be people who have no destination in mind because not knowing where you're going will slow you down. Have you ever been a little turned around while trying to find an address or a landmark? The first thing we tend to do is to slow down because we're not certain of our surroundings and have little confidence that we can get there driving with purpose at a normal speed. If not knowing where you're going will slow you down then not knowing who you are will bring you to a screeching halt. What is worse is it will cause you to travel in the wrong direction, all the while believing you're on the right path. That's true deception. The Bible tells us that knowing the truth will make us free. Free from what? The deceptions and limitations of this world system.

> *Now the serpent was more crafty than any of the wild animals the LORD God had made. He said to the woman, "Did God really say, 'You must not eat from any tree in the garden'?"* [2] *The woman said to the serpent, "We may eat fruit from the trees in the garden,* [3] *but God did say, 'You must not eat fruit from the tree that is in the middle of the garden, and you must not touch it, or you will die.'"* [4] *"You will not certainly die," the serpent said to the woman.* [5] *"For God knows that when you eat from it your eyes will be opened, and you will be like God, knowing good and evil."*
> *Genesis 3:1-5 (NIV)*

Since humanity's conception Satan has worked diligently to deceive us and steal our identity. He is operating in the same way he operated with Eve in the garden of Eden. All humanity suffered because Eve failed to see herself in the image and likeness of God, having all God's attributes and character blessed and destined to live forever.

In a moment of deception she forfeited everything because she didn't have revelation that she was already like God the Creator. God told Adam and Eve to be fruitful and multiply because they were co-creators with God, but Eve just couldn't see it. Her failure to draw her identity from God cost her everything and was quite pricey for all mankind. Eve saw her identity through the eyes of the serpent and this great deception has proven costly. Once we truly believe what the Word of God says about us our identity will began to conform to that image, this means we must reject the concept that we are what we did and accept the truth that is presented *"As He is so are we in this world" 1 John 4:17.* The bible says when we accept Christ as our Lord and Savior we become like Him. I know we tend to look at Christ and see so much natural difference that it's difficult to imagine ourselves as He is, but that is the truth. Everything that He is gets credited to our account and He has already paid the price for us to be made righteous before God.

However, it is our responsibility to replace our self-image with His. We must accept His work in place of our works and remember His work pleased the Father so now we receive that gift by faith. Furthermore, anytime we're tempted to believe some indictment about who we are based on our works we must look to Christ and say" Jesus paid for our prosperity so we're prosperous", "Jesus paid for our healing so we're healed", "Jesus was made wisdom for us so we're wise", it's already done. The only thing we should be waiting on is manifestation of these promises which comes by faith in the finished work at the cross.

We are who God said we are and it's up to us to believe it if we want to see it evidenced in the earth. A friend of mine once told me evidence defeats doubt. I believe this to be true because the Bible states that after the Word of God was preached it was followed by miracles that demonstrated the power of God. Likewise, our identity in Christ should produce evidence that The Word is true. Identity in Christ is our inheritance and it will produce evidence but only if we believe. Otherwise, all we have is the world's idea of identity based on self-effort or righteousness based on religion and that won't produce evidence. See yourself in Christ.

Is your identity in stuff?

It is quite understandable that we are proud of our accomplishments and truthfully speaking we are designed for accomplishment. However we must be ever mindful that our accomplishments by world standards can never be the center of our identity. It is very easy to adopt the world's philosophy of worth and value and make it the core of our belief system. It's actually a very subtle seduction. You slowly slip into a mindset that begins to quietly judge people depending on their situation in life and their material gains.

Slowly, but surely we begin to use that measuring stick to compare ourselves to others and when we don't feel as though we measure up we have a negative self-perception. If you feel better about yourself surrounded by those you believe are worse off than you, you have bought into the worlds value system. At that point you've slipped into the world's philosophy of value and worth and it is destructive by design.

It is quite amazing how much of our identity is cloaked in what we own and what we do. Most people, when asked who they are, will often respond with what they do. It seems our identity is so closely connected to our work or profession that we have come to see them as one in the same. However we find this to be true most often with people who are proud of what they do for a living. You'll rarely hear someone ask a janitor or dishwasher who they are and they respond with what they do. While both are respectable jobs that society can't live without, people don't typically demonstrate great pride in those jobs. Why is that? Why do some people associate themselves with their jobs more than others? They all pay currency so the only difference is the amount. So, is that it? Could it be that the pride we feel when we use our profession as our identity is actually all about money?

This idea that money somehow defines us is the foundation of the worlds value system. If you just spend enough money people will respect you. If you buy diamonds, cars, and vacations people will identify with you as a winner. You see the stuff tells the story, I recall a line from the rapper Nas. It said, "I'm out for presidents to represent me, I'm out for dead presidents to represent me", and this was a reference to money. That is the overall sentiment of society. People want money to represent them, but is it the best position to assume, making money your representative? We've been told that money is the ultimate identifier. It separates the winners from the losers.

But what is money? Why was there so much talk about it in the Bible? I have to believe there was so much talk about money because God knew we would be tempted to make a god of money. According to God's design, if we are to have an accurate self-identity we are to draw that identity from our God Jehovah and not society's god, money. However, because God gave us free will we are at liberty to make gods of anything we choose, but that's not really a good idea.

> **Don't you realize that you become the slave of whatever you choose to obey? Romans 6:16 (NLT)**

God left the decision up to us of choosing where we draw our identity from. *Chose this day who you will serve Joshua 24:15.*

These scriptures say in essence you will draw your identity from whom you serve. If you serve God you gravitate and draw your identity from Jesus Christ; adopting His attributes, His love, His viewpoint, His very identity. But if money is what we serve then we have thrust upon us all of the attributes of money as our god.

> *The blessing of the LORD, it maketh rich, and he addeth no sorrow with it. Proverbs 10:22*

According to scripture God maketh rich, but absent God it destroys and brings with it every identity destroying characteristic known to man; insecurity, jealousy, envy, greed, and strife. Not to mention you're never quite sure why your friends are around, or why people seem to like you. You don't know if people think you're funny or they laugh because you're picking up the tab.

Your identity becomes whatever society says it should be based on their definition of who they think you are. God's plan is for us to be confident and assured of who we are because we are in Christ and in Christ an exchange has taken place. All of my weakness, limitations and shortcomings have been exchanged for the excellence perfection and glory of Jesus Christ.

> *And he said unto me, My grace is sufficient for thee: <u>for my strength is made perfect in weakness.</u> 2 Corinthians 12:9*

Unlike the world, we are in Christ regardless of whether or not we have a job society believes is worth identifying with. Our prestige and honor comes from our relationship with Christ, not man. So even if we find ourselves in professions or situations that some might associate with as identity we won't falter because we understand that it's Jesus. It's His work and His grace that has put us in the position that some would call their identity. In Christ we know that He did the work and we get the benefits.

> *Bless the LORD, O my soul, and forget not all his benefits:*
> *Proverbs 103:2*

Identity can be a fragile thing for most of us because if we aren't careful the way people view us can have a huge effect on how we view ourselves. Sometimes sports programs tell the stories of athletes that at one point in life were some of the most famous faces on the planet. Interestingly enough as the stories go on inevitably they get to the part where the athlete begins to believe their own press. They know that the world loves them and they feel as though they're on top of the world, but without fail they come to the second part of the story. The parts of the story where they get injured, released, or by some other means stop making millions. All of a sudden the cameras and endorsements go in another direction and then comes the depression. When the money is gone with it goes their identity. Usually when money dries up people are viewed differently by others; others who by the way are blind themselves. Once the money is gone they see themselves negatively because they adopted the world's viewpoint and value system to define themselves.

The world's system claims that to be without money is to be without God. As we mentioned, whatever you serve will be your god and you will draw you identity from what you serve. I would suspect that money is a terrible god. However, this too is a choice.

If we consider the thing more than the creator, at the end of the day all we will have is the thing … maybe. By placing more value on God's philosophy which is to *(seek ye first the kingdom of God and righteousness in Christ having all other things be added to you)* your identity will be established and you will reign as a king in life. You can't get there without letting go of the worlds ideas of who you are and replacing them with Gods.

Self-Deception

Self-deception is defined as the act of lying to yourself or making yourself believe something that isn't really true. Self-deception is a phenomenon because it is the process of believing what we know is not true, either about ourselves or others. It's interesting that we as people can purposefully choose to believe what we know is a lie and then began to identify with and act based on that lie. Society promotes that type of thinking and is a strong advocate of the "fake it till you make it" mindset. In essence we are encouraged to pretend to be something we're not to impress people we probably don't like to make them like or respect us.

The only reason someone would want to fake it till they make it is because there are feelings of inadequacy present. Feelings of inadequacy will always be a by-product of not identifying with Christ. In Christ there is no inadequacy there is no desire to "fake it till you make it". In Christ we already have it.

> *According as his divine power hath given unto us all things*
> *that pertain unto life and godliness, 2 Peter 1:3*

It's amazing what is happening in the world and the direction it appears to be heading. For instance when we were growing up we didn't try to call what is wrong right. If you stole it was stealing and it was wrong no matter what the reason. When women or men slept around with various people it wasn't something that was viewed as a positive. There was no concept of hooking up. If you behaved that way it was something to be ashamed of, especially if you were a woman.

However, in the world's philosophy this behavior makes you "a boss" meaning you're someone in charge and in control. The agenda of Satan is to have us behave in destructive ways and then convince us that the identity associated with the behavior is something to be desired. That's just plain foolishness. It's been said that a rose by any other name is still a rose, and no matter what the world wants to call something, those of us in Christ should know exactly what it is. It's self-deception. I once heard someone say "people love to be lied to", that's why fantasy movies are so popular. That's not to say that all fantasy movies are bad but it does illustrate the fact that we love to engage in make believe. We choose to believe anything that is said often enough and we employ no effort to determine its validity.

Self-deception requires us to convince ourselves of something regardless of its truth and regardless of any facts or evidence to the contrary. No matter how many stories we hear about the evils of a wrong relationship with money, society still believes that money alone is the answer. If we'd just pay attention we would see the deception in that and we would recognize that the people who are most happy with wealth and material things have a right relationship with money. These people understand that God gives increase and gives us the power to gain wealth. Money and things can never provide us an accurate identity.

Our identity in Christ can provide money and things but we won't fall prey to our self-deception. It is our identity in Christ that will strip away self-deception, self-effort and boasting and the Word of God will expose any temptation we may have in this area.

> *But my God shall supply all your need according to his riches in glory by Christ Jesus. Philippians 4:1*

In Christ there are riches and glory and these riches won't conflict with the identity that Christ provides for believers.

Chapter 3

WHO TOLD YOU THAT?

Most of us have found that there have been people in our lives who have been a blessing to us. These people have encouraged us when we were down; they spoke hope and confidence to us. They reassured us that we could do anything we could put our minds to, but the truth be told, most of us didn't get enough of that to tip the scales in favor of a positive self-image. However, on the other hand, there was never any shortage of nay-sayers; people who were absolutely certain you were going to be just like your no-good . . . you fill in the blank. You know those people who felt it was their duty to "keep it real" and "tell you like it is", which was nothing more than their opinion. People are willing to shatter a dream or curse a life with their mouths, and worse yet, they help make seeing yourself as God see's you a real battle. Therefore, we must always consider who is saying what. It matters (*who told you that*).

Things you may have heard along the way. The good, bad, and ugly

Many believers say that everything that happens is either God's will or God has allowed it, but the truth is that God gave mankind dominion and authority over the earth back in the Garden of Eden. Along with that dominion and authority, we have responsibility to enforce God's laws on the planet. (His Kingdom Come His Will be done on Earth as It Is in Heaven) Religion has thoroughly taught us that God is in control and everything that happens on earth is somehow His plan. It is true that God is Sovereign but in His sovereignty He chose to give control of earth to man for a period of time.

> *And <u>God said, Let us make man in our image, after our likeness: and let them have dominion</u> over the fish of the sea, and over the fowl of the air, and over the cattle, and <u>over all the earth</u>, and over every creeping thing that creepeth upon the earth. Genesis 1:2*
>
> *The heaven, even the heavens, are the LORD's: but the earth hath he given to the children of men. Psalm 115:1*

Just think about that for a moment. God gave the earth to us to manage. You may have never heard this before because it is a somewhat radical revelation and not aligned with traditional religious teaching. Something else not aligned with religious teaching is the idea that our identity comes from Jesus Christ and we are not to see ourselves as a sum total of our actions be they good or bad. When we accept Jesus as our savior, our sins are forgiven; past, present and future.

> ^{12} whereas Christ, having offered the one sacrifice [the all-sufficient sacrifice of Himself] for sins for all time, SAT DOWN [signifying the completion of atonement for sin] AT THE RIGHT HAND OF GOD [the position of honor],
>
> ^{14} For by the one offering He has perfected forever and completely cleansed those who are being sanctified [bringing each believer to spiritual completion and maturity].
>
> Hebrews 10:12, 14 (AMP)

The idea that we are in any way unworthy before God is incorrect. Our identity before God the Father is that of God the Son. Imagine if we accepted Jesus Christ as our savior, but never chose to strip off the old man through the renewing of our minds in the Word of God. We would be saved from hell but would probably live a very frustrated life while on earth. Failure to renew our minds will leave us with the mindset and identity of the world even though we are saved and have access to everything God has to offer. We would still have a mind filled with insecurity, past failures and identity crisis. There is a more glorious side to this. When we chose to renew our minds in The Word, the Bible says that we have the mind of Christ. If that's not a new identity I could not tell you what is. The identity associated with the idea that God is in control and causes everything that happens leaves us with the identity of a puppet in the game of life. If that were true, what would be the point of prayer, giving or going to church at all?

If God in His Sovereignty had already decided what would happen no matter what you did, why bother with the Christian walk? If God were in control of everything, that would make Him responsible for every premature death, every natural disaster, every disease, all poverty and every famine. That would even make Him responsible for the disobedience in the Garden of Eden. Therefore, Him being in control independent of man is simply not accurate. Can you imagine not knowing if God was for you or against you. What kind of identity do you believe that would manifest in believers? You don't have to imagine. You can actually visit most of the churches in America any given Sunday morning and you will see for yourself the identity this type of thinking produces.

Earlier we stated that evidence defeats doubt and is proof positive of a seed being sown. When you see the evidence of powerless saints who don't know who they are; you actually see the evidence of the seed of doubt or unbelief. Our identity in Christ provides the Blood bought right to call things that aren't as if they are! This new identity allows us to use God's power and authority as if we were Jesus Himself. This power we utilize is the same power that raised Christ from the grave. This power that enables us to be transformed into the image of Christ is a direct by-product of the great exchange provided by Jesus at the cross. He exchanged His riches for our poverty, His stripes for our healing, and His perfect relationship with the Father for our estranged relationship. When we see ourselves in Christ it not only produces an accurate perception of ourselves, but provides the power to put His identity on, like a garment to do what He did in the earth.

> *Verily, verily, I say unto you, He that believeth on me, the works that I do shall he do also; and greater works than these shall he do; because I go unto my Father. John 14:12*
>
> *For as many of you as have been baptized into Christ have put on Christ. Galatians 3:27*
>
> *I can do all things through Christ which strengtheneth me. Philippians 4:13*

Lies of the enemy

> *Ye are of your father the devil, and the lusts of your father ye will do. He was a murderer from the beginning, and abode not in the truth, because there is no truth in him. When he speaketh a lie, he speaketh of his own: for he is a liar, and the father of it. John 8:44*

What we believe will essentially determine our journey as well as our destination. Right believing will produce right living, and the believing we speak of as right believing is believing the truth in the Bible regarding God, Jesus and ourselves. We wanted to emphasize the distinction between right believing and wrong believing because what you believe will determine your destination and identity. As we've mentioned, your identity is how you view yourself. Wrong believing will produce the wrong picture and as a result wrong living. Just as right believing (**God's Word**), will produce the right picture and right living. We define right living as the application of God's principles to bring about the best possible results in every area of human life. We believe every person on the planet desires the results that right living can produce.

However, the majority of people will never know the best possible result, because our believing is incorrect and the wrong picture produced by wrong believing will produce struggle, strife, lack, sickness and an identity of defeat and despair.

What we believe matters and the only way to detect a lie is to know the truth and the Word of God is truth. Please understand also, that the Word of God is not the only voice present. We have an adversary (the devil) and he desires to deceive us into wrong believing so that we produce the wrong picture and in turn the wrong identity producing the wrong results. Why does Satan want us to see ourselves inaccurately? Because he knows that an inaccurate picture will produce results that create discouragement, doubt, unbelief and impotency. Where these mindsets exist there is no power because there is no faith.

So now, what are some of the tools tricks and lies the enemy uses to get us to believe wrong and produce the wrong self-image? Well, we must begin with the truth that Satan is a liar. As a matter of fact the Bible states (**he is the father of lies**). We can expect for him to lie to us about everything. One of the biggest lies Satan uses is that we should be afraid, but afraid of what? Afraid that our sins and short comings have put distance between us and God.

If we believe this lie, we won't expect the Word of God to produce any good results in our lives. He wants us to believe the Blood of Jesus did not pay our, past, present and future sin debt. However, the Word of God says the sacrifice of Jesus paid for our past, present and future sins. **Hebrews 10:12**

Now that's truly the good news but only if you believe this Gospel of God's Grace.

> [12]*whereas Christ, having offered the one sacrifice [the all-sufficient sacrifice of Himself] for sins for all time, SAT DOWN [signifying the completion of atonement for sin] AT THE RIGHT HAND OF GOD [the position of honor .*
>
> [14] *For by the one offering He has perfected forever and completely cleansed those who are being sanctified [bringing each believer to spiritual completion and maturity]*
>
> [17] *"AND THEIR SINS AND THEIR LAWLESS ACTS I WILL REMEMBER NO MORE [no longer holding their sins against them]."*[18] *Now where there is [absolute] forgiveness and complete cancellation of the penalty of these things, there is no longer any offering [to be made to atone] for sin. Hebrews 10:12,14,17,18 (Amp)*

Satan wants us to believe because we have sinned we are not righteous before God. That attack on our righteousness is really two fold. First he wants to discredit the work of the Blood of Jesus. Second, he wants to attack our identity in Christ. The Bible says Jesus was made righteousness for us.

> *But it is from Him that you are in Christ Jesus, who became to us wisdom from God [revealing His plan of salvation], and righteousness [making us acceptable to God], and sanctification [making us holy and setting us apart for God], and redemption [providing our ransom from the penalty for sin], 1 Corinthians 1:30 (Amp)*

That's very important because we received our righteousness from the work of Jesus not our own performance. Because His performance was perfect and because we are in Christ, God sees us as perfect, highly regarding everything that Jesus did and crediting our account just as though we did the work ourselves.

> *For God made Christ, who never sinned, to be the offering for our sin, so that we could be made right with God through Christ. 2Corinthians 5:21 (NLT)*

Another lie that Satan employs to attack our identity is to tell us everything has not been done, that the work of the cross is not finished. He wants you to believe that there are things God has promised, but you will just have to wait and see if God will do them. This couldn't be further from the truth. The Bible states that God did everything before the foundation of the earth. .

> *God chose him as your ransom long before the world began, but he has now revealed him to you in these last days. 1Peter1:20 (NLT)*

God worked for six days and on the seventh day He rested, not because He was tired but because His work was all finished.

Then the Lord said to me, "You have seen well, for I am [actively] watching over My word to fulfill it." Jeremiah 1:12 (Amp)

For instance, healing has already been completed. The Bible tells us we are healed past tense.

> *But he was wounded for our transgressions, he was bruised for our iniquities: the chastisement of our peace was upon him; and with his stripes we are healed. Right now! Isaiah 53:5*

If Satan can convince us that we are the sick hoping to get healed versus being healed already, he has effectively attacked our identity as people who have already been healed. Satan also wants us to believe in the concept of lack. He wants us to believe it's not God's will to prosper believers financially, however the word of God states:

> *It is God that gives us the power to get wealth. Deuteronomy 8:18*
>
> *Let them shout for joy, and be glad, that favour my righteous cause: yea, let them say continually, Let the LORD be magnified, which hath pleasure in the prosperity of his servant. Psalm 35:27*

One of Satan's most effective lies is that he wants us to believe deliverance only comes if we can somehow keep all the law that was brought by Moses. *For sin shall not have dominion over you: for ye are not under the law, but under grace. Romans 6:14*

We are in Christ with Jesus' sacrifice credited to our account, the law has already been fulfilled and met through the work of Jesus. We are in Christ and He is in us. Because of Him we are no longer under the Law of Moses. We are now under the Law of Grace through the New Covenant which came by Jesus. The Bible states that Jesus is full of grace and truth, John1:14 KJV. So guess what, because of Him we are filled with grace and truth. Again it's not by our works, but His.

Another trick used to rob us of an accurate view of our identity is to foster and develop this mindset; that if we do good we get good and if we do bad we get bad.

> *Or do you have no regard for the wealth of His kindness and tolerance and patience [in withholding His wrath]? Are you [actually] unaware or ignorant [of the fact] that*
>
> *God's kindness leads you to repentance [that is, to change your inner self, your old way of thinking—seek His purpose for your life]? Romans 2:4 (AMP)*

This mindset puts all the focus on us and creates a pattern of self-effort to attempt to please God. Truth be told, no amount of self-effort will ever please God. We absolutely need a savior The Bible tells us that if we violate in just one area of the law (self-effort) we have effectively violated all of the laws.

For the person who keeps all of the laws except one is as guilty as a person who has broken all of God's laws. James 2:10 (NLT)

Therefore, it's clear why Satan will promote this kind of thinking. He knows that *Jesus is the only way to righteousness.* If he can get us to believe we can be righteous through our own power, we will make the work of Jesus of no effect in our lives. Believing this lie will distort our identity because if we fail time and time again it has a detrimental effect on faith and identity. The Word of God is our only source for discovering our godly heritage and the only source for detecting the lies of the enemy.

There is a battle for our minds and there is only one place where we can see ourselves accurately; that is in the truth of the Word of God.

What I say doesn't matter

We as believers must understand the power of our words. As speaking spirit's made in the likeness and image of God, we have the ability to speak and activate earthly laws.

> *I will worship toward thy holy temple, and praise thy name for thy lovingkindness and for thy truth: for thou hast magnified thy word above all thy name. Psalm 138:2*
>
> *Who being the brightness of his glory, and the express image of his person, and upholding all things by the word of his power, when he had by himself purged our sins, sat down on the right hand of the Majesty on high: Hebrews 1:3*

The entire world is held together with God's words and we must understand that God has given us the power to use His words to create the life He wants us to have on earth. That means that if we believe, we'll have what we say.

> *Thou shalt also decree a thing, and it shall be established unto thee: and the light shall shine upon thy ways. Job 22:28*
>
> when ye pray, believe that ye receive them, and ye shall have them. *Mark 11:24*

Satan would like for us to disregard this truth because he knows that if we're ignorant to this truth we will fail to see ourselves as co-creators made in the image and likeness of God. He has no problem with us saying what we feel or what we think unless of course it's the Word of God. You see, the Word of God will never return void and it will always produce God's results. Likewise, if we choose to say something other than what God has said, we work this law in reverse; either way we will have what we say. It's the law.

The Bible says our tongues can speak blessings or curses and that's important because often times we speak without regard for what God has said about a matter. What is a blessing and what is a curse? A blessing is any statement that lines up with the Word of God and a curse is any statement that opposes the Word of God. When God said we are healed, we say that we are healed. When God said that we are blessed, we say we're blessed. When God says that we're prosperous and we look at our bank book and say with great conviction that we are broke, then we are cursing our finances. When the doctor gives us a bad report we shouldn't call everyone we know and tell them our death is imminent. That's cursing our health and it's in opposition to the Word of God. Remember we will have what we say.

41

The proper response in all situations is necessary to see the promises of God come to pass in our lives. Regardless of how we feel about a matter we are to speak The Word only. God is not obligated to manifest anything He has not promised. The Bible says that He will watch over His words to perform them. He will not alter anything He has spoken. It's our responsibility to say what He has said instead of saying anything that opposes what He has said. His only responsibility is to honor His words and even then He needs our co-operation.

We must open our mouths and declare what He has established. We are speaking spirits for a reason, and the reason is to establish His kingdom in the earth.

Without saying something we effectively slow the process of manifesting His power to all men. God's desire is that all of His children demonstrate His love and power so all men can see the goodness of God. We are to be a walking talking advertisement for the Kingdom of God, however no one will want what we have if it doesn't produce results. Going forward let us pray we develop sensitivity to the things we say so that our witness will draw men to Christ. If we sound as though we're struggling and believe like the world, our proclaimed identity in Christ won't be attractive to anyone because it will appear as powerless religion.

We must declare our righteousness in Christ daily. We must command the promises of God be made manifest in our lives. We must decree and declare we are healed and prosperous in Jesus' name. When we replace the curses with The Blessing we will walk in the manifested power of Jesus and our identity in Christ will be a witness to all.

"Death and life are in the power of the tongue, and those who love it will eat its fruits."

Proverbs 18:21

"I tell you, on the day of judgment people will give account for every careless word they speak, for by your words you will be justified, and by your words you will be condemned."
Matthew 12:36-27

"Let no corrupting talk come out of your mouths, but only such as is good for building up, as fits the occasion, that it may give grace to those who hear." Ephesians 4:29

"There is one whose rash words are like sword thrusts, but the tongue of the wise brings healing." Proverbs 12:18

Chapter 4

GOD SAID

We often hear people quote scriptures from the Word of God and that's a wonderful thing because Gods word is truth. However, it is important to understand what God said in its proper context. There is a very big difference between what we could expect as believers before The Cross versus after the cross. Prior to Jesus dying for our sins we were under the Law that came by Moses and it was simple, do good and you'll get good. Do bad and you'll get bad; however The Bible states that the Law was perfect, so it was mankind that was the problem. As a matter of fact the Law was called the *ministration of death* in 2 Corinthians 3:7 and that was because no man could keep the Law and the wages of sin is death. However, after the cross we entered into the New Covenant: the covenant of grace whereby we see the amazing grace of God by faith. The Blood of Jesus changed how we operate.

For Christ is the end of the law for righteousness to everyone that believeth. Romans 10:4

We no longer have to view our actions as the determining factor of our righteousness. According to the new covenant Jesus did all the work. God made Jesus to be righteousness for us 1Corinthians1:30. No longer was self-effort or our abilities considered as righteousness. That's a game changer because now we know that whenever we come to God we can come boldly to His throne with the assurance that we are in right standing with God. **Hebrews 4:16**

This new identity in Christ gives us confidence that faith in this assurance is well placed because Jesus did it all for us. He qualified us and all we have to do is believe.

Now when we look at the Word of God wherever we see a conditional blessing such as" if you keep my commandments" and we began to reflect on our actions we can look to Jesus who is the author and finisher of our faith and know the every requirement has been met.

> *And lo a voice from heaven, saying, This is my beloved Son, in whom I am well pleased . Matthew 3:17*

Now that we have our (*saved by grace through faith*) glasses on let's take a look at some of the promises that the precious Blood of Jesus has made available to those who believe.

> *For God so loved the world, that he gave his only begotten Son, that whosoever believeth in him should not perish, but have everlasting life. John 3:16*

So Christ has now become the High Priest over all the good things that have come. He has entered that greater, more perfect Tabernacle in heaven, which was not made by human hands and is not part of this created world. [12] With his own blood—not the blood of goats and calves—he entered the Most Holy Place once for all time and secured our redemption forever.

Just think how much more the Blood of Christ will purify our consciences from sinful deeds so that we can worship the living God. For by the power of the eternal Spirit, Christ offered himself to God as a perfect sacrifice for our sins.
Hebrews 9:11-12 &14 (NLT)

It is because of him that you are in Christ Jesus, who has become for us wisdom from God--that is, our righteousness, holiness and redemption 1Corinthians:1:30 (NIV)

But now apart from the law the righteousness of God has been made known, to which the Law and the Prophets testify
Romans 3:21 (NIV)

God made him who had no sin to be sin for us, so that in him we might become the righteousness of God. 2 Corinthians 5:21

For Christ has already accomplished the purpose for which the law was given. As a result, all who believe in him are made right with God. Romans 10:4 (NLT)

But to him that worketh not, but believeth on him that justifieth the ungodly, his faith is counted for righteousness. Romans 4:5

For I know the plans I have for you, declares the Lord, plans to prosper you and not to harm you, plans to give you hope and a future. Jeremiah 29:11 (NIV)

And my God will meet all your needs according to the riches of his glory in Christ Jesus. Philippians 4:19

Worship the Lord your God, and his blessing will be on your food and water. I will take away sickness from among you, Exodus 23:25 (NIV)

The Lord is my shepherd, I lack nothing. He makes me lie down in green pastures;
He leads me beside quiet waters. Psalm 23:1-2 (NIV)

Meditate on these words until they saturate you heart and spirit and release them from your mouth. This is who we are in Christ Jesus. This is our identity under the new covenant.

Chapter 5

THE CHOICE IS YOURS

For some readers I am sure much of this comes as a shock, and perhaps it seems to be in opposition to what you've learned from religion. However, this is The Gospel of Grace; The Good News of Jesus Christ. We have been reconciled back to God! Now, I need to make this clear, this is not a "*License to sin*". Meaning the Grace of God should not be taken advantage of as an opportunity to sin. Although sin will not be imputed to us sin will have natural consequences that can make life much harder than it has to be. As we renew our minds in the Word of God His grace and the Holy Spirit will empower us to live the life God desires for His children.

Since creation of mankind, God has given us a choice. We get to decide what we believe, and with that we get to decide what our identity will be. We are the only creation made in the image and likeness of God and we were made with the power to make decisions. We get to choose even the minute details of our lives, from what we want to wear to where we want to live. Deciding where we draw our identity from is no minute detail. It's the most important decision we will ever make. In most areas of life there are many options, but in this area of identity there are but two. We will either decide on purpose to draw our identity from God or by default we will be forced to draw our identity from the world's viewpoint with its values, traditions and mindsets.

Many of us had no intention on gravitating to the world's system of worth and value, but this happens by default. We get to choose what we are hearing and receiving in terms of negative messages regarding how we view ourselves. We are not just ole' sinners saved by grace.

We are the new creation in Christ.

Brothers and sisters in Christ we get to choose, and considering all that we have covered by now the choice should be simple.

If we adopt the world's philosophy of identity then we can expect a life of confusion, failure and frustration. However when we choose God we get to draw our identity from Christ Jesus and all things become possible.

Thank you again, and our prayer is that this book will in some way help each and every reader to better understand who they are in Jesus Christ. He is the King of Kings and Lord of Lords and we and Christ are one.

> *But he that is joined unto the Lord is one spirit 1Corinthians 6:17*
>
> *I am crucified with Christ: nevertheless I live; yet not I, but Christ liveth in me: and the life which I now live in the flesh I live by the faith of the Son of God, who loved me, and gave himself for me. Galatians 2:20*

Call to Salvation

Our prayer is that the revelation regarding who you are in Christ is clear and convincing. The Word of God is truth and as that truth begins to take hold in your heart we believe that God will constantly reveal the truth of your identity.

Contrary to popular belief no one goes to hell because of sin. People go to hell because they reject the payment for their sins that has been provided as a free gift by God.

We prayerfully encourage you to accept the gift of no condemnation offered through the death, burial, and resurrection of Jesus Christ. You can receive eternal life right now by believing in your heart and confessing with your mouth that Jesus Christ is Lord.

> *⁹ That if thou shalt confess with thy mouth the Lord Jesus, and shalt believe in thine heart that God hath raised him from the dead, thou shalt be saved.*
>
> *¹⁰ For with the heart man believeth unto righteousness; and with the mouth confession is made unto salvation. Romans 10:9-10*

Just say, Father, I come to you thanking you for the gift of salvation through the death, burial and resurrection of Jesus. I accept Jesus as my savior and lord by faith and I am now the righteousness of God through His sacrifice on the cross, amen.

About The Authors

Angela Kinnel is a professional educator and Robert Johnson is President of a Christian based manufacturing company. They are both anointed believers and share a deep thirst for the gospel of grace. They met while attending World Changers Bible School and reside in the Atlanta Georgia area.

Biography

Angela Kinnel

Angela Kinnel is a 10 year veteran educator. A native Georgian, she was born in Dawson, Georgia. She is currently a student at World Changers Bible School in College Park, Georgia. Angela resides in Hampton, Georgia.

Robert Johnson

Robert Johnson, is a native of Chicago, and currently resides in Georgia. Robert is the father of 3 and has been married for 29 years to Debra. He is currently attending World Changers Bible School to further his pursuit of the truth in the Word of God.

Identity

For More Info Contact: www.bloodboughtpromises.com

Notes

Notes

Notes

Notes

www.ingramcontent.com/pod-product-compliance
Lightning Source LLC
Chambersburg PA
CBHW060708030426
42337CB00017B/2805